Flower Patterns

To Appliqué, Paint, and Embroider

D1533116

JOAN   SJUTS   WALDMAN

Located in Paducah, Kentucky, the American Quilter's Society (AQS) is dedicated to promoting the accomplishments of today's quilters. Through its publications and events, AQS strives to honor today's quiltmakers and their work and to inspire future creativity and innovation in quiltmaking.

Editor:	Lee Jonsson
Book Design/Illustrations:	Chad Murray
Cover Design:	Chad Murray
Photography:	Charles R. Lynch

Library of Congress Cataloging-in-Publication Data

Waldman, Joan Sjuts.
    Flower patterns: to appliqué, paint, and embroider / Joan Sjuts Waldman.
    p. cm.
    ISBN 1-57432-726-7
    1. Machine quilting–Patterns. 2. Appliqué–Patterns. 3. Textile painting. 4. Flowers in art.
    I. Title.

TT835.W3334   1999
746.46041–dc21   99-048083

Additional copies of this book may be ordered from the American Quilter's Society, PO Box 3290, Paducah, KY 42002-3290 @ $19.95. Add $2.00 for postage and handling. www.AQSquilt.com

Copyright © 2000, Joan Sjuts Waldman

All rights reserved. No part of this book may be reproduced, stored in any retrieval system, or transmitted in any form, or by any means including but not limited to electronic, mechanical, photocopy, recording, or otherwise, without the written consent of the author and publisher. Patterns may be copied for personal use only.

Contents

Acknowledgments

A big thank you goes to my husband Harold,
who very patiently supports me in everything I attempt to do.

To the members of the Calico Quilt Club,
who are always willing to try a new idea, and also encourage me
to push the limits just a little farther.

To my children, Cynthia, Randall, and Erick,
who during their growing years, put up with a mother
with a needle in her hand.

To Brenda Groelz,
for permission to share her no-fail method of joining bias binding.

To Hari Walner,
for inspiring me to venture into trapunto quilting by machine.

To Rose Cattau,
for loaning me photographs of her wonderful iris garden.

To AQS,
for seeing possibilities in the watercolor-pencil painting technique.

To my editor Lee Jonsson,
for organizing the content of this text.

To Chad Murray,
for the wonderful cover/book design and illustrations.

To Charles R. Lynch,
for photography.

Introduction

The concept for this book grew out of the watercolor-pencil painting technique described on the following page. You will see how versatile this technique is when you see it combined with appliqué, embroidery, and trapunto, and used on a wonderful assortment of flower blocks and labels.

Each section of the book describes one of six different techniques. Following the descriptions are projects that incorporate the techniques. As the book progresses and techniques are added, they are also combined, giving you a chance to try something new and expand your creative options.

How It Began

Watercolor-pencil painting developed quite by accident. I was at a convention and chanced to overhear a conversation between two doll makers. One remarked that she used watercolor pencils on her doll faces, wet the color, then heat set it to make the color permanent. (At the time, I didn't think to ask questions or inquire who the ladies were.)

A few years went by. I had drawn a set of flower patterns with the intention of making appliqué blocks. The overheard conversation popped back into my mind and I thought I would try to color them with watercolor pencils.

The first attempt at using the watercolor pencils was almost the last. I drew a flower on a piece of fabric, colored it, and dipped it in water. Whoosh! It bled all over the background and ran off the bottom of the block. Still, I liked the color that resulted, so I decided to try again. The next time, I used a small, soft paintbrush to wet the color. The results were better, but it still allowed too much water on the watercolor. The next try, I used a stiff paintbrush, and pressed out almost all the water. Ah-ha! Much better results.

I took the block to my quilt club. Everyone was excited about the technique, so I worked up a class sheet and we had a class. With the success of those first pencil paintings, I knew this relatively unexplored technique was on its way to becoming a book.

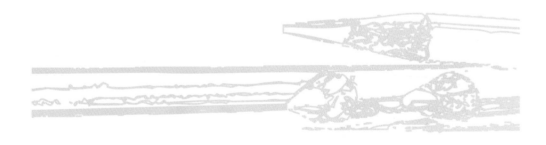

Watercolor-Pencil Painting

The watercolor-pencil painting technique described in this book has evolved from that first attempt. It is a lot of fun, and you can achieve good results with minimal time and expense. So, dig out some muslin, fabric pens, and watercolor pencils and dive into the joy of making watercolor-pencil-painted pictures.

To get started you will need a hair dryer, an iron, and the following supplies:

Fabric for the blocks:

A good-quality, bleached cotton muslin works best. Wash, dry, and press the fabric before you start to paint. Cut the fabric slightly larger than the finished block size. You will trim the block after the painting is completed.

Fabric Pen:

A black .01 fabric pen works well for most designs. If you have a set of colored fabric pens, you can match the pen color to the color you will use for the flower. The outlines must be made using a permanent marker. If an ordinary pen is used, it may run when the water is applied to the watercolor, thus ruining your design.

Fabric Medium or Textile Medium:

This product is found with acrylic paint supplies in discount and hobby stores. Mix ⅓ fabric medium to ⅔ water to help set the watercolor and keep it from fading.

Watercolor Pencils:

Many different brands are available. I have tried several and every brand seems to work well. Art supply stores carry many different sizes of pencil sets. To begin, a set of 24 will be sufficient to work the blocks in this book. If you decide later that you want to expand your color range, sets of 48 and more are available.

If you live in an area where there are no convenient art stores, many catalogs offer mail-order service. These are reliable sources:

The Artist's Club
P.O. Box 8930
Vancouver, WA
98668-8930
(800) 845-6507

Dick Blick Art Materials
P.O. Box 1267
Galesburg, IL
61402-1267
(800) 828-4548

Jerry's Artarama
P.O. Box 58638J
Raleigh, NC
27658
(800) 827-8478

ASW Express
5325 Departure Drive
North Raleigh, NC
27616-1835
(800) 995-6778

Sax Arts & Crafts
P.O. Box 510710
New Berlin, WI
53151
(800) 323-0388

Directions

Center the prepared block over a pattern. Trace the pattern with a .01 fabric pen. Heat set the outline using your iron turned to the setting that matches your fabric, e.g., cotton. Now you are ready to paint.

Begin by "painting" the leaves in your design. Choose the darkest green or teal in your pencil set. Stroke around the outline of the leaves. Do not press hard on the pencil; build layers by gently stroking color on each leaf or stem (Photo 1). Work strokes in the direction that leaves grow – from the tip, down, and from the base of the leaf, up.

Photo 1. Paint leaves first, building layers of color.

The next step is to gradually blend the next lightest color over the inside edge of the darker color (Photo 2). Continue to blend lighter greens toward the center of the leaf. (This gives the leaf the look of being rounded.) Finish by using a yellow-green to lightly highlight the center of the leaf (Photo 3). Finish all the leaves and stems.

For variety, you can reverse the shading – using the darkest color in the center and the lightest on the outer edges.

The next step is to decide what colors you want for your flowers.

Photo 2. Gradually blend lighter colors over inside edge of darker colors.

Photo 3. After leaves are painted, add highlights for realism.

Look in gardening books or take photographs of flowers to get a feel for what colors to use for different flowers. Flower catalogs have many pictures that will also suggest colors to use in your flower blocks. For example, irises come in almost all colors and combinations of colors. Some have color only on the edges of the petals and some are brilliantly colored. You can shade your flowers from dark to light or from light to dark. The following instructions are for dark to light.

The same technique is used to color the petals on the flowers. Start at the base or center of the flower and around the edges of the petals with the darkest shade used. If you want to use a single color, shade the outside edges of the petals darker than the petal centers (Photo 4). When all the petals of the flowers are painted, you are ready to blend the colors with liquid.

Photo 4. Shade outside edges of blossoms darker than center.

There are several ways to apply the fabric medium/water mixture: one way is to use a stiff paintbrush; another way is to use a cotton swab; however, the best way is to put the mixture in a spray bottle. You may want to test different bottles to find one that puts out a very fine mist. Avoid spray bottles that produce drops of mixture because that can make the sprayed area look blotchy. I have had good results with eyeglass cleaner spray bottles and small travel-size hair spray bottles. The easiest way to mix the fabric medium and water is to pour the container of fabric medium into the spray bottle (if it is large enough) and add two containers of water. Shake the spray bottle to mix the solution each time you use it.

To begin blending your design, lay the pencil-colored fabric on a newspaper covered with paper towels, or an old terry cloth towel that you do not mind getting color on. Hold the spray bottle about six inches from the fabric. Quickly mist the design with the fabric medium/water mixture. This will blend the colors. Experiment on a sample piece to get the feel of how much moisture is necessary to get the blending without excessive bleeding outside the pen lines. Some bleeding outside the lines will occur.

If you use a stiff paintbrush or cotton swab to wet the design, mix the fabric medium/water solution and pour a small amount into a shallow dish. Dip the brush or swab into the dish and squeeze out the excess moisture. Gently stroke the design with the damp brush or swab. It takes a lot more time to blend the colors using the paintbrush or swab, and it is easy to get too much liquid on the fabric and cause excessive bleeding. However, these applicators work well if you want to blend a small area or if an area needs more color. Simply apply the color and re-wet that area to blend the color.

immediately after you finish wetting it directs any excess water onto the design and prevents the color from bleeding outside the pen lines. When the block is completely dry, heat set with the iron.

The next step is to add fine pen lines around the design for definition. You can also make little squiggly lines in the background of the design area. I usually choose to do this in green. Add detail lines to the design using either a matching or contrasting color pen. When you are satisfied with the way the block looks, take a light- to medium-green watercolor pencil and lightly stroke the area behind the flowers. Lightly spray the block with the fabric medium/water mixture and dry. Heat set the whole block, then trim to the exact block size and you are ready to put it in your quilt top.

Since watercolor-pencil painting will fade after repeated launderings, I do not recommend using this technique on a child's quilt or on anything that will be laundered frequently.

Photo 5. Completed block.

When you have finished wetting the block, use a hair dryer to dry the surface of the block. Point the dryer from the outside of the design to the inside. Drying the block

Flowers of Spring
41½" x 41½"

This wall quilt uses five of my favorite flower blocks: the tulip, iris, poppy, lily, and morning glory. You can choose any five flowers that you like for this quilt. The flower blocks are watercolor painted. If you want them to stand out, you can add trapunto before setting them into the top.

Flower Patterns ✳ To Appliqué, Paint, and Embroider   Joan Sjuts Waldman

Flowers of Spring

Fabric Requirements (All yardage based on 45"-wide fabric.)

⅔ yard muslin

2⅜ yards print fabric for setting triangles, outer border, and backing

¾ yard accent fabric for flower block frames, inner border, and binding

43" square piece of batting

Cutting Instructions (Cut strips selvage to selvage.)

Painted blocks:
Five 11" squares of the muslin fabric (trimmed to 10½" when finished)
Six 1" strips of the accent fabric to frame the flower blocks

Setting triangles:
Two 9" squares of the print fabric for the corner triangles
One 17" square of the print fabric for the side triangles

Borders:
Four 4" strips of the print fabric for the outer border
Four 1½" strips of the accent fabric for the inner border

Finishing:
One 43" square of the print fabric for the backing
Four 2¼" strips of the accent fabric for the binding

Directions (Use ¼" seam allowance for piecing.)

Flower patterns begin on page 81. Using the watercolor-pencil painting technique described on pages 6–9, trace the flower patterns on the 11" muslin blocks and heat set. Color, wet, dry, and heat set the designs. Add trapunto to the flowers if you want them to stand out from the background. (See pages 62–63 for information on trapunto.) Trim the blocks to 10½".

Sew the 1" accent strips around the painted squares (Fig. 1).

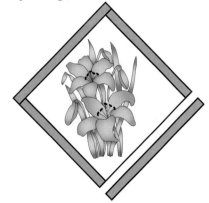

Figure 1. Use 1" accent fabric strips to frame each flower block.

Flowers of Spring

For the setting triangles, draw a line diagonally across the 9" print squares. Sew a line of stay stitching ⅛" from each side of the drawn line (Fig. 2). Cut on the drawn line.

Draw a line diagonally across the 17" print square in both directions. Sew a line of stay stitching ⅛" from the drawn lines (Fig. 3). Cut on the drawn lines.

Arrange the blocks and setting triangles as shown in the diagram (Fig. 4). Make sure the flowers have the correct orientation, with stems down.

After piecing the center, trim edges to allow for a ¼" seam allowance around the entire top (Fig. 5).

Figure 4. Assembly diagram.

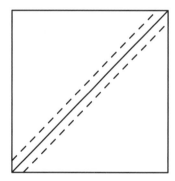

Figure 2.
Preparing corner setting triangles.

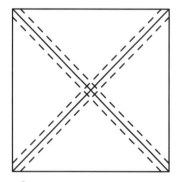

Figure 3.
Preparing side setting triangles.

Figure 5. Trim pieced top, leaving ¼" seam allowance past block points.

Add the 1½" inner border strips to the sides, then to the top and bottom. Trim any extra length. Add the 4" outer borders to the sides, then to the top and bottom (Fig. 6). Trim.

Figure 6. Add inner and outer borders, first to sides, then top and bottom.

Layer the backing, batting, and top. Using 1" quilting safety pins, pin securely around trapunto areas and then approximately 4" apart in the background areas. Machine quilt in all the seam lines. Add additional quilting designs as desired.

Bind the quilt. (See pages 79–80 for information on binding.) Make a label and attach it to the back of the quilt. (See page 94 for information on labels.)

Flowers at the Crossroads
73½" x 85½"

The flower blocks in this quilt are watercolor-pencil painted,
and stitched with trapunto. I used the wrong side of the fabric
for the pieced blocks so they would not be too bright
and overpower the flower blocks.

Flowers at the Crossroads

Fabric Requirements (All yardage based on 45"-wide fabric.)

4 yards bleached muslin
1½ yards green fabric
3 yards print fabric
5⅜ yards backing
1 full-size package of cotton batting

Cutting Instructions (Cut strips selvage to selvage.)

Painted blocks:
Fifteen 13" squares of bleached muslin (trimmed to 12½" when completed)
Seven 4½" strips of green fabric cut into sixty 4½" squares

Pieced blocks:
Seven 4½" strips of bleached muslin cut into sixty 4½" squares
Two 4½" strips of print fabric cut into fifteen 4½" squares
Eight 2½" strips of bleached muslin
Eight 2½" strips of print fabric

Borders:
Eight 5½" strips of print fabric

Finishing:
Two panels 40" x 89½" for backing
Eight 2¼" strips of green fabric for the binding

Directions (Use ¼" seam allowance for piecing.)

Flower patterns begin on page 81. Enlarge patterns 135% for this quilt. Using the watercolor-pencil painting technique described on pages 6–9, trace the enlarged flower patterns on the 13" muslin blocks and heat set. Color, wet, dry, and heat set the designs. Add trapunto as desired. (See pages 62–63 for information on trapunto.) Trim blocks to 12½" when finished.

Prepare corners for the painted blocks by drawing a diagonal

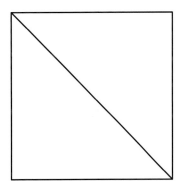

Figure 7. Mark sewing line to prepare corners for painted blocks.

Flowers at the Crossroads

sewing line on the back of the 4½" squares (Fig. 7).

With right sides together, place one green square on each corner of a 12½" block and sew on the marked diagonal line. Trim corner to ¼" from the seam line (Fig. 8). Press toward green. Make fifteen flower blocks (Fig. 9).

For pieced blocks, sew one muslin and one print strip together. Repeat eight times. Press toward the print fabric. Cut these strip sets into 120 2½" x 4½" strips (Fig. 10). Sew these strips into four-patch blocks (Fig. 11).

Arrange the four-patch blocks, muslin squares, and print squares as shown (Fig. 12).

Figure 9. Finished painted block.

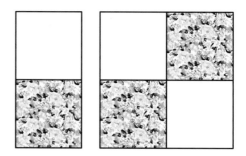

Figures 10 & 11. Strip sets and four-patch block.

Figure 8. Trim away excess corner fabric, leaving ¼" past seam line.

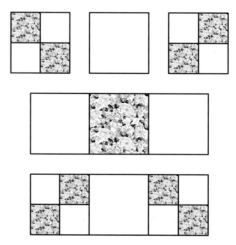

Figure 12. Pieced block assembly.

Flowers at the Crossroads

Figure 13. Finished pieced block.

Figure 14. Quilt assembly.

Piece the squares into rows, and the rows into blocks. Make fifteen blocks (Fig. 13).

Arrange the painted flower blocks and pieced blocks as shown (Fig. 14). Piece the blocks together into rows. Piece the rows together to make the center of the quilt.

For the borders, sew the eight 2½"-wide green strips end to end. Sew the border to the sides of quilt center. Trim. Press. Sew the border to the top and bottom of quilt center. Trim. Press.

Sew the eight 5½"-wide strips of print fabric end to end. Sew the border on the sides of the quilt. Trim. Press. Sew the border on the top and bottom of the quilt. Trim. Press.

To assemble the quilt, sew the backing panels together on one long edge. Layer the backing, batting, and top. Using 1" quilting safety pins, pin the layers together approximately 4" apart. Machine quilt in the seam lines, between the blocks, and around the borders. Sew a line of stay stitching ⅛" from the edge of the quilt. Evenly trim backing, batting, and top.

Quilt around the flowers. Quilt across the pieced blocks. Quilt the scallop in the flower blocks and the leaf design in the muslin squares of the pieced block. Quilt the borders.

Sew the eight 2¼"-wide strips of green fabric end to end. Press in half lengthwise. Bind the quilt. (See pages 79–80 for information on binding.) Make a label and attach it to the back of the quilt. (See page 94 for information on labels.)

Flowers at the Crossroads
Full-size quilting patterns

Use in green corner triangles that frame flower blocks.

Use in white muslin squares.

Flower Patterns ❋ To Appliqué, Paint, and Embroider   Joan Sjuts Waldman

Watercolor-Pencil-Painted Appliqué

Watercolor-pencil painting can also be done on appliqué blocks. The painting technique combined with the three-dimensional quality of appliqué enhances the life-like look of these flowers.

To get started you will need a set of watercolor pencils, fabric for the appliqué pieces and blocks, a fabric pen, a spray bottle of fabric medium/water solution, a hair dryer, and an iron.

Directions

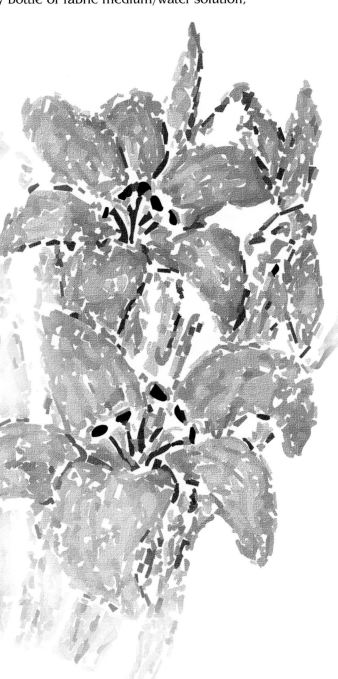

Using a .01 black fabric pen, trace the appliqué pattern pieces on good-quality, bleached cotton muslin. Leave at least ½" between pieces. This will allow for seam allowances.

Color the appliqué pieces with the appropriate watercolor pencils. The darkest color pencil should be used around the outside edge of the appliqué piece. The lightest color pencil should be used in the center of the appliqué piece. Gently stroke the fabric with the pencil to build up the color. Do not try to apply all the color needed with one stroke of the pencil. Continue shading until you like the look of the leaf or petal. Hint: Use the side of the pencil for better control with shading. Follow this same procedure with all the appliqué pieces.

The next steps are to wet the appliqué pieces with the fabric medium/water, dry them with a hair dryer, and heat set them as described on pages 8–9.

Now you are ready to cut out your pieces and appliqué them to a background. Cut around each piece, leaving a ¼" seam allowance.

Paper-Baste Appliqué

There are many different ways to appliqué. My favorite way is to paper-baste. For this method, trace each appliqué pattern piece on paper. (I use sheets of paper from bulk mail.) Cut out the pattern with a paper scissors exactly on the drawn line. Pin the paper to the wrong side of your watercolor-painted piece of fabric. I pin from the back (Fig. 15). Cut out the fabric piece, leaving a ³⁄₁₆" turn-under allowance by eye.

Take basting thread, knot the end, and begin basting on top of the piece. (The knot will be on top of the fabric.) Work the allowance to the back of the paper and baste in place with medium stitches, every ½"–¾" inch. When you come to a point, fold the end over and then work the sides over the fold to create a sharp

point (Fig. 16). Baste only the edges of the pieces that will be on top. If a portion of the pattern piece will fall under another piece, do not turn or baste that edge. It will be covered by another appliqué piece.

I use unit appliqué. This means I appliqué pieces together into units before stitching them to the background. For this method, start with the piece that will be on top and appliqué it to the allowance of the piece it will cover (Fig. 17). Assemble as much of the design as possible. Then position the whole unit on the background fabric. Pin from the back with short pins. Then appliqué the unit into place on the block. If you have a problem working with the pins on the back of the fabric, you can baste the whole unit to the background, then appliqué.

Sew the appliqué to the background with a blind stitch. To blind stitch, select thread that matches

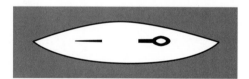

Figure 15. Pin paper pattern piece to wrong side of fabric.

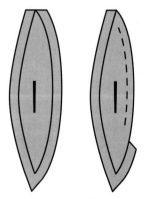

Figure 16. Turn the allowance to the back and baste.

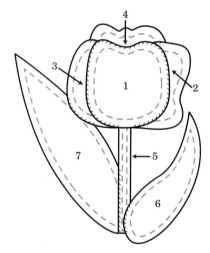

Figure 17. For unit appliqué, assemble the design in layers, beginning with the pieces that are on top.

the appliqué pieces. Knot the thread. Bring it up through the fabric, and just catch one or two threads of the appliqué. Pull the thread through. Slip the point of the needle under the appliqué, back down through the background fabric, close to the place where you came up. Then, come up under the edge of the appliqué about ¹⁄₁₆"–⅛" from the first stitch. Again, catch one or two threads of the appliqué. Repeat until you have appliquéd all but ½" of the piece. At this point, clip the basting knot and pull the basting thread out. Next, reach under the appliqué piece with a tweezers and grasp the paper, pull the paper out, and finish sewing the piece to the background (Fig. 18).

An alternate method of removing the paper is to complete the appliqué,

remove the basting, make tiny slits in the background fabric behind the appliqué, and pull the paper pieces out with tweezers. The small slits in the background can be whip stitched, or they can be left unstitched because the quilting will stabilize the fabric.

Freezer-Paper Appliqué

Another common appliqué method is freezer-paper appliqué. This method works in much the same way as paper-baste appliqué. The pattern is drawn on the freezer paper, cut out, and the shiny side of the paper is pressed to the back of the appliqué pieces. (Remember to trace the pieces in reverse on the dull side of the freezer paper and press to the back of the appliqué pieces.) Cut out the fabric, adding approximately ³⁄₁₆" seam allowance. Instead of basting, needle-turn the seam allowance around the paper as you stitch each piece into units. When the appliqué is complete, make tiny slits in the background behind the appliqué pieces and pull the paper out with tweezers.

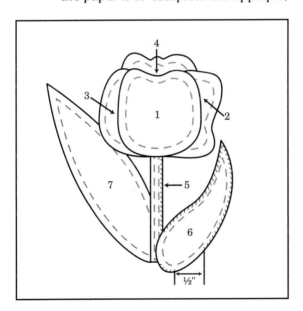

Figure 18. Sew appliqué to background with blind stitch; pull out paper pattern through a ½" opening.

Free-Form Basting Appliqué

In this method, the appliqué piece is drawn on the fabric. Allow approximately a ³⁄₁₆" seam allowance when cutting the pieces out. Turn the seam allowance under and run a basting thread near the marking line. Press when seam is basted. Appliqué into units and then appliqué the units to the background. When you are finished, remove all the basting thread.

Lilies in Appliqué
19" x 21"

The lily pattern, page 88, was made using watercolor-painted fabric for appliqués. Never again will you have to search for that perfect color for an appliqué piece. You simply color the fabric, wet, dry, and heat set. Then, cut out the desired piece and appliqué in place.

Lilies in Appliqué

Fabric Requirements (All yardage based on 45"-wide fabric.)

½ yard (or a fat quarter) of the background fabric for the center panel
½ yard bleached muslin for the appliqué pieces
1¼ yards contrasting fabric for the border, binding, and backing
21" x 23" piece of cotton batting

Cutting Instructions (Cut strips selvage to selvage.)

Painted panel:
One 13" x 15" muslin block for center panel
Trim to 12½" x 14½" when appliquéd

Border:
Two 3½" strips for the border

Finishing:
One 21" x 23" block for the backing
Three 2¼" strips for the binding

Directions (Use ¼" seam allowance for piecing and ³⁄₁₆" turn-under allowance for appliqué.)

The lily pattern on page 88 was used for this quilt, but you can use any of the patterns on pages 82–93. Enlarge your chosen pattern 150% for this quilt. Trace individual petals and leaves on muslin blocks with a fabric pen; heat set. Allow ½" between pieces for seam allowances. Using the watercolor-pencil painting technique described on pages 6–9, color, wet, dry and heat set the appliqué pieces. Cut out the appliqué pieces, allowing a ³⁄₁₆" turn-under allowance around each piece. Turn under the allowance and baste. Appliqué the pieces in units as described on pages 20–21.

Trim the panel edges as needed. Sew the border strips to the sides of the center panel, then to the top and bottom of the center panel.

Layer the backing, batting, and top. Using 1" quilting safety pins, pin the layers together. Stitch around the border. Quilt around the appliqué. Quilt ⅛" from the edge of borders. Quilt a design in the border.

Bind the quilt. (See pages 79–80 for information on binding.) Make a label and attach it to the back of the quilt. (See page 94 for information on labels.)

Lilies in Appliqué
Full-size border pattern

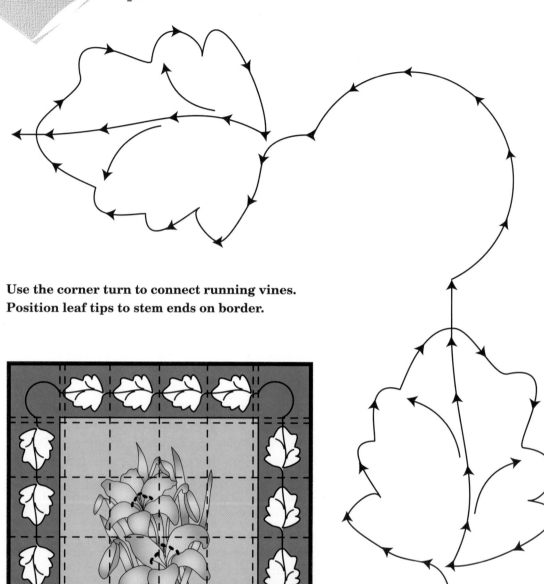

Use the corner turn to connect running vines.
Position leaf tips to stem ends on border.

Figure 19. Border quilting design.

Free-Form Machine Embroidery

Free-form machine embroidery is another way to embellish a quilt. Because this technique is done after the quilt top, batting, and backing are put together, machine embroidery not only adds color and design to the quilt, but also secures the three layers of the quilt.

You will need a water-soluble marker, water-soluble stabilizer, small pins, and a variety of colored thread.

Directions

Once the quilt is basted, thread the machine on top with your desired color, such as green for leaves and stems. Thread the bobbin to match or blend with the quilt backing. Set the machine for darning, that is, the feed dogs should be down or covered, and the darning foot should be on the machine.

To begin, trace the design with the marker on the stabilizer. Pin the stabilizer on the block using small pins. Stitch over the tracing on the lines. Go over the lines several times to build up the design (Fig. 20).

When starting a row of stitching, position the machine needle where you want to begin. Let the needle go up and down several times in place, then move very slowly for three to five stitches. Gradually move the fabric so the stitching follows the lines of the design. As you approach the end of a stitching line, move the fabric very slowly for a few stitches, and then let the needle go up and down in the same place for another several stitches. This will secure the end so you can cut the thread without tying off.

Figure 20. Stitching several times over the traced lines of a design builds up the design.

Wildflowers
23" x 23"

For this quilt, I did some rough sketches of wildflowers and later drew the designs found here. All of the flower blocks have been machine embroidered.

Wildflowers

Fabric Requirements (All yardage based on 45"-wide fabric.)

4 fat quarters dark plaid
4 fat quarters light plaid
⅜ yard accent fabric for the inner border and binding
½ yard plaid fabric for the outer border
¼ yard bleached muslin
¾ yard backing fabric
25" square of cotton batting
Water-soluble stabilizer, water-soluble markers, assorted colored thread for embroidery.

Cutting Instructions (Cut strips selvage to selvage.)

Painted blocks:
Nine 4¼" squares of bleached muslin
Nine 4¼" squares of water-soluble stabilizer

Nine-Patch blocks:
Twenty 1¾" squares of dark plaids
Sixteen 1¾" squares of light plaids

Setting triangles:
Four 5" squares of light and dark plaids
One 5½" square of plaid

Borders:
Two 1¼" strips of accent fabric for the inner border
Three 3½" strips of plaid for the outer border

Finishing:
One 25" square for the backing
Three 2¼" strips of accent fabric for the binding

Directions (Use ¼" seam allowance for piecing and ³⁄₁₆" turn-under allowance for appliqué.)

Piece four Nine-Patch blocks using the 1¾" squares (Fig. 21). For the side triangles, draw a line diagonally across each 5" square. Sew a line of stay stitching ⅛" from each side of the drawn line (Fig. 22). Cut on the drawn lines.

Figure 21. Nine-Patch block.

Wildflowers

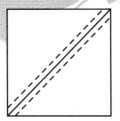

Figure 22. Prepare side triangles from 5" squares. Prepare corner triangles from 5½" squares.

Figure 23. Quilt assembly diagram. Piece by diagonal rows, adding corner triangles last.

Figure 24. Trim quilt, leaving a ¼" allowance, measured from block points.

For the corner triangles, draw a line diagonally across the 5½" square in both directions. Sew a line of stay stitching ⅛" from the drawn lines (Fig. 22). Cut on the drawn lines.

Arrange the Nine-Patch blocks, the muslin blocks, and the triangles as shown. Assemble the quilt top in diagonal rows (Fig. 23). Piece row 1, then lay it back into position. Continue until all five rows are sewn and repositioned. Add the triangles to row 1 and row 5. Then sew all the rows together. Press the top. Trim the edges ¼" from the block points (Fig. 24).

Sew the inner border to the sides of the quilt. Trim the extra length even with the quilt's edges. Sew the inner border to the top and bottom. Trim.

Sew the outer border to the sides. Trim. Then sew the outer border to the top and bottom. Trim.

Press the top. Layer backing and batting, then center the top on the batting. Using 1" quilting safety pins, pin the layers together. Machine quilt in all seam lines and around the borders. Sew a line of stay stitching ⅛" from the edge of the border.

Trace the wildflower designs on the water-soluble stabilizer with a water-soluble marker. Center the design on one of the bleached muslin squares. Pin in place, using several small pins. Embroider the design, using the instructions on page 25. When you are finished, unpin and tear the stabilizer away from the stitching. Put the piece into warm water to dissolve the rest of the stabilizer. Squeeze the excess water from the quilt, lay it on several layers of toweling, and block. Leave to dry for about an hour.

With watercolor pencils, lightly touch the areas of flowers and leaves. This will leave just a hint of color on the blocks. When completely dry, press with an iron. (Press lightly, not with full pressure on the iron.) Touch the colored areas with a cotton swab moistened with a fabric medium/water mixture. Dry with the hair dryer and, again, press lightly.

You can then quilt around the flowers and quilt a design in the pieced blocks and triangles as desired. A sample quilting motif is included. For more information on designing a quilting pattern, see pages 68–69.

Bind the quilt. (See pages 79–80 for information on binding.) Make a label and attach it to the back of the quilt. (See page 94 for information on labels.)

Quilting design for border triangles.

Full-size wildflower pattern.

Wildflowers

Full-size wildflower patterns

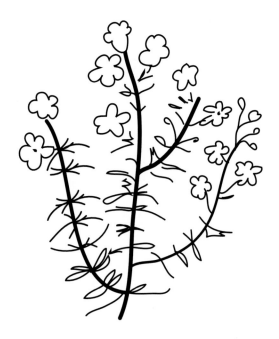

Flower Patterns ✳ To Appliqué, Paint, and Embroider   Joan Sjuts Waldman

Wildflowers
Full-size wildflower patterns

Watercolor-Pencil/Embroidery Quilts

The idea for this type of watercolor quilt came from an antique quilt, which was stenciled and had embroidered details. The blocks looked like they had been appliquéd with embroidery stitches. These blocks can be either embroidered or appliquéd. (Appliqué instructions start on page 19.)

Directions

Using the watercolor-pencil painting technique described on pages 6–9, trace the flower patterns on the blocks and heat set. Color, wet, dry, and heat set the designs.

Choose embroidery floss that is just a shade darker than the colors used in your designs. Work a stem stitch (Fig. 25) or chain stitch (Fig. 26) around each detail in the design.

Figure 25. Stem Stitch

Right-handed   Left-handed

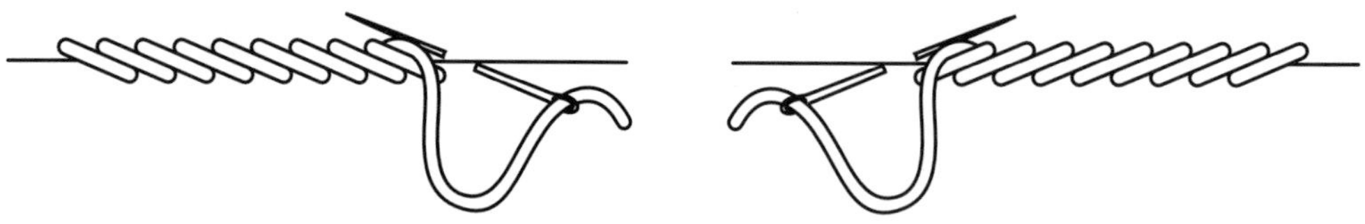

Keep thread below line of stitching while working.
Bring needle up at the midpoint of the stitch.
Notice that stitches slant across the line.

Figure 26. Chain Stitch

Right-handed   Left-handed

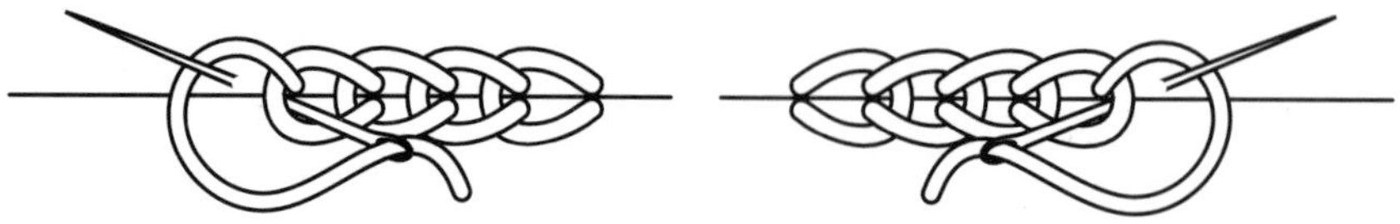

To end the chain stitch, bring needle up in center of last loop,
and down outside that loop to back of fabric.

Baltimore Bride's Quilt
36" x 36"

I have always wanted to make a Baltimore Bride's quilt. This pattern was designed so I could actually do one. The blocks were colored, then embellished with an outline stitch around the designs.

Baltimore Bride's Quilt

Fabric Requirements (All yardage based on 45"-wide fabric.)

1¾ yards unbleached muslin for the blocks, borders, and binding
1¼ yards backing
39" square of cotton batting
Embroidery floss in deeper shades than the colors used for the designs

Cutting Instructions (Cut strips selvage to selvage.)

Painted blocks:
Sixteen 7" blocks of muslin (trim to 6½" after being completed)
Border:
Four 7" strips of muslin for the border (trim to 6½" after being completed)
Finishing:
Four 2¼" strips of muslin for the binding

Directions (When piecing use a ¼" seam allowance unless otherwise specified.)

Center and trace the designs on the 7" muslin blocks and heat set. Using the watercolor-pencil painting technique described on pages 6–9, color, wet, dry, and heat set the design. Embroider the outlines in a slightly darker shade of embroidery floss than the color used to paint the designs. You can use either a stem stitch or a chain stitch (Figs. 25–26, page 32).

Piece the blocks to make the center of the quilt. Sew a border strip to each side of the quilt. Trim. Press. Sew a border strip to the top and bottom. Trim. Press.

Next, trace the floral border designs on the border and heat set. Color as desired, wet, dry, and heat set. Embroider the outlines of the border designs.

Layer the backing, batting, and top. Using 1" quilting safety pins, pin the layers together. Quilt around the designs.

Bind the quilt. (See pages 79–80 for information on binding.) Make a label and attach it to the back of the quilt. (See page 94 for information on labels.)

These blocks can also be appliquéd, if you prefer. Trace the pieces given for each block on muslin and heat set. Using the watercolor-pencil painting technique described on pages 6–9, color, wet, dry, and heat set the design. Then cut out the appliqué pieces, adding a ³⁄₁₆"–¼" seam allowance for each piece. Appliqué the pieces into units and then appliqué the units on the background.

The stems are ¾" strips of bias. Fold the bias in half lengthwise and stitch a scant ⅛" seam from the raw edge. Cut the lengths needed for each block. Lay the folded edge over the raw edge and appliqué into place. If the ends are not hidden under another appliqué piece, finish them by turning them under and appliquéing them into place.

Baltimore Bride's Quilt
Full-size pattern

Oversized blocks will be trimmed to 6½" after being appliquéd.

Baltimore Bride's Quilt
Full-size pattern

Flower Patterns ❀ To Appliqué, Paint, and Embroider   Joan Sjuts Waldman

Baltimore Bride's Quilt
Full-size pattern

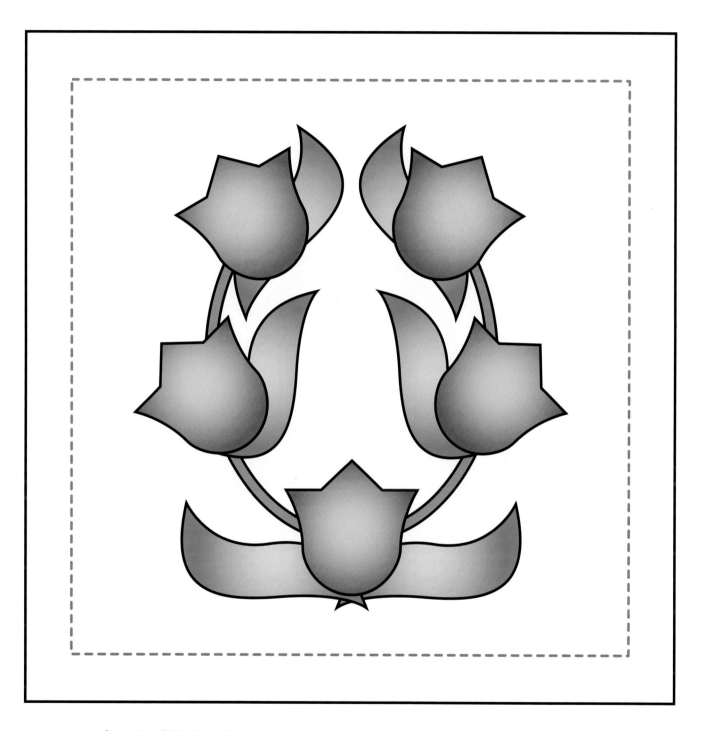

Oversized blocks will be trimmed to 6½" after being appliquéd.

Baltimore Bride's Quilt
Full-size pattern

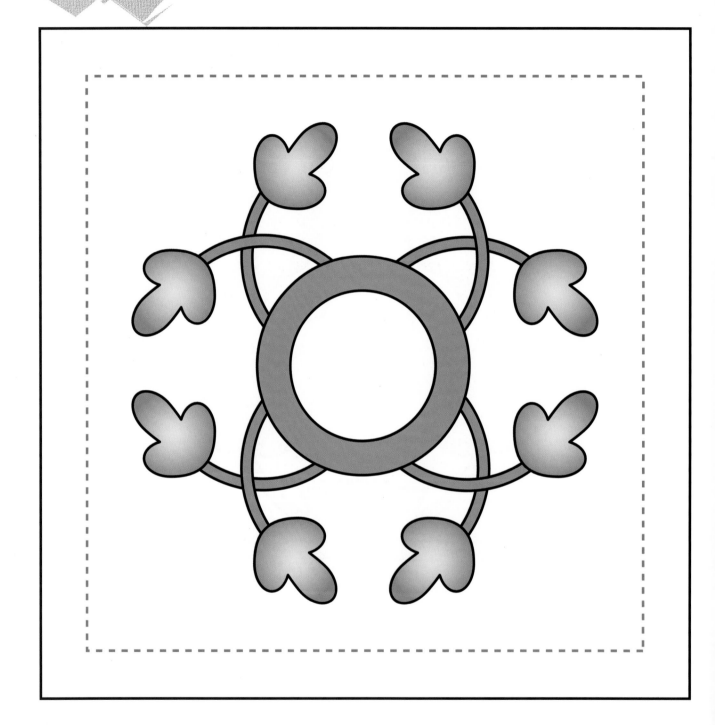

Flower Patterns ❋ To Appliqué, Paint, and Embroider   Joan Sjuts Waldman

Baltimore Bride's Quilt
Full-size pattern

Oversized blocks will be trimmed to 6½" after being appliquéd.

Baltimore Bride's Quilt
Full-size pattern

Flower Patterns ❋ To Appliqué, Paint, and Embroider   Joan Sjuts Waldman

Baltimore Bride's Quilt
Full-size pattern

Oversized blocks will be trimmed to 6½" after being appliquéd.

Baltimore Bride's Quilt
Full-size pattern

Baltimore Bride's Quilt

Full-size pattern

Oversized blocks will be trimmed to 6½" after being appliquéd.

Baltimore Bride's Quilt
Full-size pattern

Baltimore Bride's Quilt
Full-size pattern

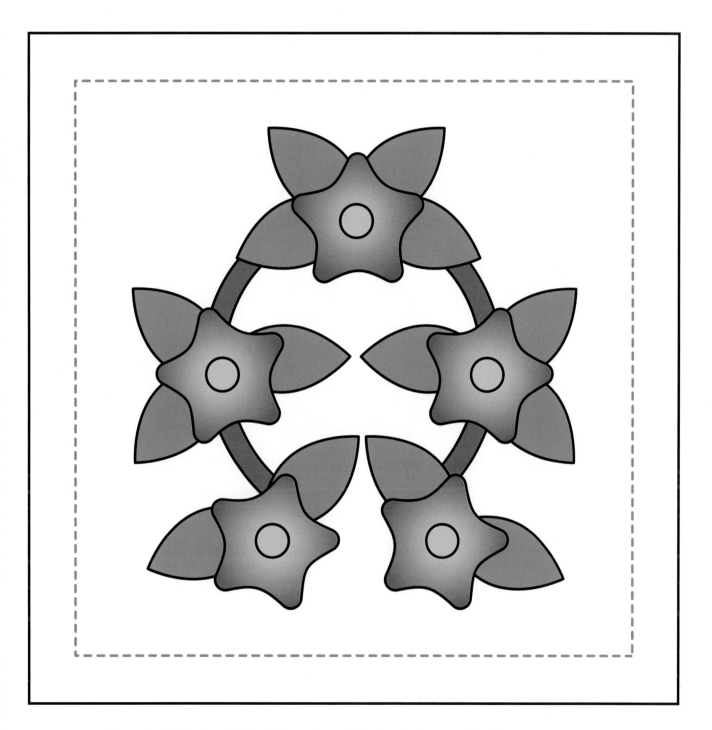

Oversized blocks will be trimmed to 6½" after being appliquéd.

Baltimore Bride's Quilt
Full-size pattern

Flower Patterns ✳ To Appliqué, Paint, and Embroider   Joan Sjuts Waldman

Baltimore Bride's Quilt
Full-size pattern

Oversized blocks will be trimmed to 6½" after being appliquéd.

Baltimore Bride's Quilt
Full-size pattern

Flower Patterns ✳ To Appliqué, Paint, and Embroider   Joan Sjuts Waldman

Baltimore Bride's Quilt

Full-size pattern

Oversized blocks will be trimmed to 6½" after being appliquéd.

Baltimore Bride's Quilt
Full-size pattern

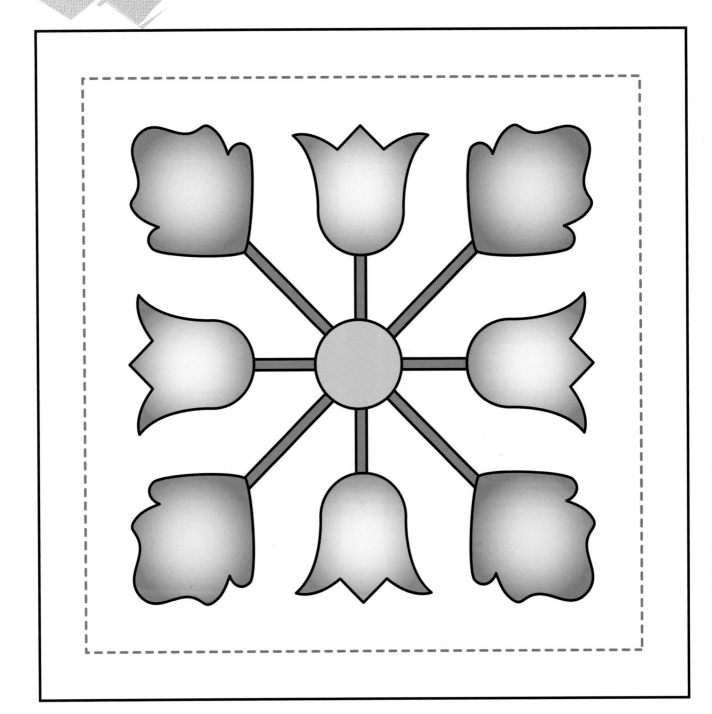

Flower Patterns ✳ To Appliqué, Paint, and Embroider   Joan Sjuts Waldman

Baltimore Bride's Quilt
Full-size border corner pattern

Baltimore Bride's Quilt

Full-size border side pattern
Position motifs and add bias stems and leaves as desired

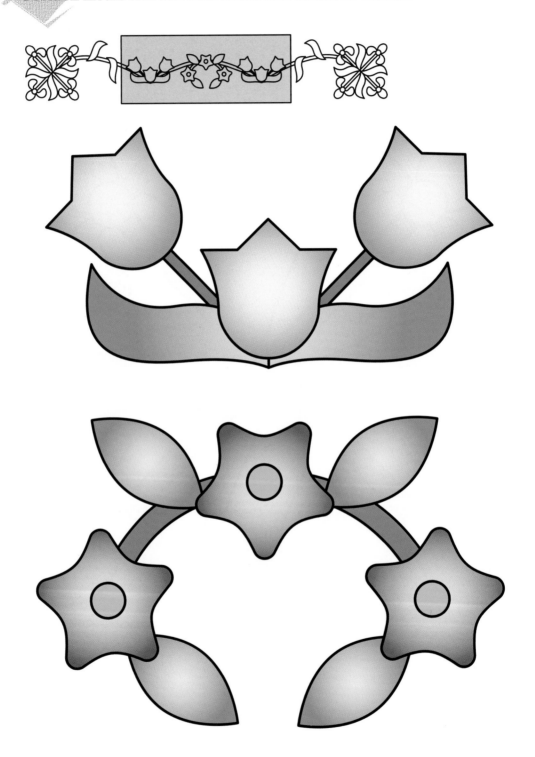

Flower Patterns ✳ To Appliqué, Paint, and Embroider   Joan Sjuts Waldman

Mrs. Cattau's Iris Garden
80" x 88"

Quilted by Dee Augustin, Shelby, Nebraska

This quilt is named for Mrs. Rose Cattau. She graciously lent me her photo albums with pictures taken in her beautiful iris gardens. These photos inspired the colors used to create the block in Mrs. Cattau's Iris Garden.

Mrs. Cattau's Iris Garden

Fabric Requirements (All yardage based on 45"-wide fabric.)

4⅜ yards bleached muslin
3¾ yards green
5½ yards backing
Queen-size package of batting

Cutting Instructions (Cut strips selvage to selvage.)

Painted blocks:

Nine 16" x 19" muslin blocks (trimmed to 15½" x 18½" when finished)

Sashing:

Twelve 2½" strips of muslin
Twenty-four 1¾" strips of green
Two 5" strips of green cut into sixteen 5" squares

Borders:

Seven 3" strips of muslin for the inner border
Eight 6" strips of green for the outer border

Finishing:

Two panels 42" x 92" for the backing
Nine 2¼" strips of green for the binding

Directions (Use a ¼" seam allowance for piecing.)

To make an iris quilt in this setting, you can use leaves and flowers (enlarged 150%) from the Misty Iris pattern, pages 66–67, and/or the iris pattern (enlarged 200%) on page 87. Alternatively, you can enlarge any of the flower patterns on pages 82–93 to 200%. Cut out the individual pieces and arrange them as you like to fit a 15" x 18" block. Trace the arrangement to make a master pattern. Use a fabric pen to trace the master pattern on nine muslin blocks; heat set. Using the watercolor-pencil-painting technique described on pages 6–9, color, wet, dry, and heat set the design.

For the sashing, sew a 1¾" green strip on each side of a 2½" white strip. Press seam allowances toward the green. Cut six strip sets into twelve 18½" slices. Cut six strips into twelve 15½" slices (Fig. 27).

Figure 27. Cut the sashing strips into slices; 12 will measure 18½" and 12 will measure 15½".

Mrs. Cattau's Iris Garden

Piece four rows: 5" square, 15½" sash, 5" square, 15½" sash, 5" square, 15½" sash, 5" square. Piece three rows: 18½" sash, block, 18½" sash, block, 18½" sash, block, 18½" sash (Fig. 28). Sew the pieced rows together to make the center of the quilt.

Figure 28. Piece even rows of squares and sashes.

Add the white inner border strips to the sides of the quilt. Trim. Press. Add the white inner border strips to the top and bottom of the quilt. Trim. Press. Add the green border in the same manner (Fig. 29).

Figure 29. Quilt assembly.

Note: The iris blocks can be trapunto quilted before assembly, if desired (pages 62–63).

Layer the backing, batting, and top. Using 1" quilting safety pins, pin the layers together, and quilt around the designs.

Bind the quilt. (See pages 79–80 for information on binding.) Make a label and attach it to the back of the quilt. (See page 94 for information on labels.)

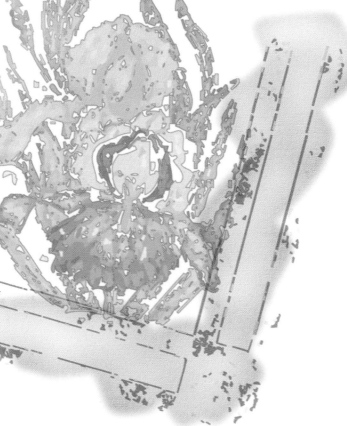

Mini-Medallion Quilt
20" x 24"

This mini-medallion was inspired by a basket block on an old 1800s quilt. The flowers from the basket were used on the borders.

Flower Patterns ✳ To Appliqué, Paint, and Embroider   Joan Sjuts Waldman

Mini-Medallion Quilt

Fabric Requirements (All yardage based on 45"-wide fabric.)

1 yard bleached muslin (includes backing and binding)

Cutting Instructions (Cut strips selvage to selvage.)

Two 22" x 26" panels of bleached muslin for the front and back of the quilt
Three 2¼" strips of muslin for the binding
One 22" x 26" piece of cotton batting

Directions (Use a ¼" seam allowance for piecing.)

Use a photocopier to enlarge the pattern 150%. Find the center of the front panel by folding it in half and then in fourths. Center the basket design on the front panel and trace with a fabric pen. Trace the border sections around the center basket with a fabric pen and heat set.

Using the watercolor-pencil painting technique described on pages 6–9, color, wet, dry, and heat set the design. If you would like to add trapunto to the design, sew a layer of extra-loft batting behind the design and then trim the excess batting. (See pages 62–63 for information on trapunto.)

Layer the backing, batting, and top. Using 1" quilting safety pins, pin the layers together. Quilt around the designs. In the center of the quilt, around the basket, and inside the border, quilt a close stipple design. Outside the border, quilt a larger stipple design. When the quilting is completed, trim to 20" x 24".

Bind the quilt. (See pages 79–80 for information on binding.) Make a label and attach it to the back of the quilt. (See page 94 for information on labels.)

Mini-Medallion Quilt
Upper-left pattern, enlarge 150%

Flower Patterns ✸ To Appliqué, Paint, and Embroider   Joan Sjuts Waldman

Mini-Medallion Quilt
Upper-right pattern, enlarge 150%

Mini-Medallion Quilt
Lower-left pattern, enlarge 150%

Flower Patterns ✳ To Appliqué, Paint, and Embroider   Joan Sjuts Waldman

Mini-Medallion Quilt
Lower-right pattern, enlarge 150%

Machine Trapunto

Trapunto is a technique that will make your design look dimensional when completed. This method of trapunto uses the sewing machine instead of the traditional method of hand sewing and stuffing the designs.

You will need water-soluble thread, a darning foot on your sewing machine, and extra-loft batting.

Water-Soluble Thread: This unique thread can be used in the sewing machine, but dissolves in water. It is available in fabric stores in most areas. Remove the thread from the sealed package and use at once. When not in use, store the thread in a resealable plastic bag. If left unsealed for long periods of time, exposure to high humidity can cause the thread to become brittle.

If you are unable to find water-soluble thread, you can use invisible thread; however, you will have to be extra careful to quilt directly on top of the first line of stitching when the whole quilt is layered and quilted.

Directions

Use water-soluble thread on the top of the machine and regular, white, sewing thread in the bobbin.

Cut a piece of extra-loft polyester batting a little larger than the design you want stuffed. Baste it in place with a few large stitches.

Drop or cover the feed dogs and put the darning foot on the machine. Place the block under the darning foot and stitch the outline of the design (Fig. 30). Do not stitch any details at this point; just stitch around the outer edge of the design. The stitching must meet to enclose the design. The details will be added after the quilt is assembled.

Next, trim the excess batting from the back of the motif. Use a blunt end scissors. (I prefer the small, blunt, children's scissors available at supermarkets, and discount and drug stores.) Carefully trim all the excess batting from the outside of the stitching (Fig. 31). This will take some time. Do not

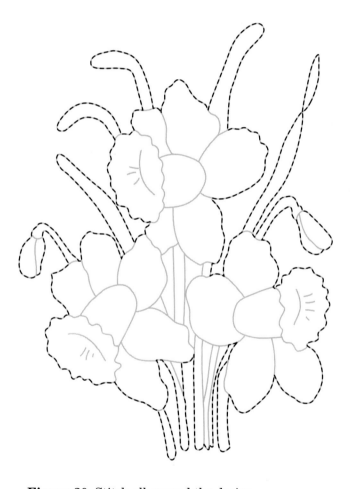

Figure 30. Stitch all around the design.

hurry the process. If you clip the fabric, you may not be able to salvage the block.

When all the areas to be stuffed have been sewn and trimmed, you are ready to assemble the quilt top. Each quilt in the book has different assembly instructions, so construct the top according to the directions. Layer the backing, batting, and quilt top. Pin the layers together. Thread the machine with regular sewing thread. Machine quilt over the water-soluble thread and over all the details of the block. Quilt around each leaf and flower petal and on any detail lines you want to emphasize. For more details on machine quilting see pages 77–78.

Once you have finished quilting, wet the quilt to remove the water-soluble thread.

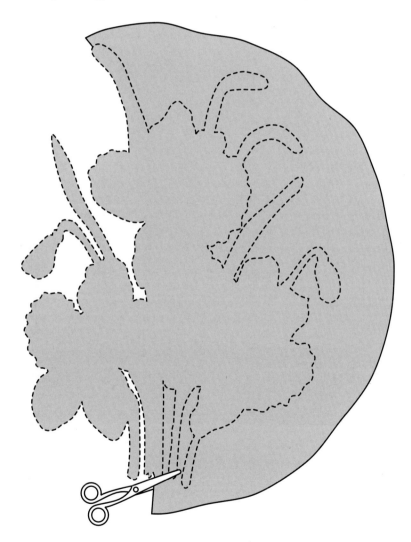

Figure 31. Carefully trim away excess batting after outlining the design.

Misty Iris
19" x 22"

Misty Iris was the first design I created with the watercolor-pencil-painting technique. This quilt inspired all the ideas for the projects in this book.

Misty Iris

Fabric Requirements (All yardage based on 45"-wide fabric.)

⅔ yard bleached muslin
½ yard print fabric for the borders and binding
20" x 23" piece of cotton batting
Scraps of extra-loft batting for trapunto

Cutting Instructions (Cut strips selvage to selvage.)

One 14" x 17" block muslin for background (trimmed to 13½" x 16½" when finished)
Two 3½" strips of print fabric for the border
Three 2¼" strips of print fabric for the binding
One 21" x 24" piece of muslin for the backing

Directions (Use a ¼" seam allowance for piecing.)

Trace the iris design on the muslin block with a fabric pen and heat set. Using the watercolor-pencil painting technique described on pages 6–9, color, wet, dry, and heat set the design. Add detail lines to flowers and background. Press again to heat set.

Add the border strips to the sides of the quilt. Trim. Press. Add the border strips to the top and bottom of the quilt. Trim. Press.

To add the trapunto, layer batting behind the flower section and stitch around the design. (See pages 62–63 for more information on trapunto.) Trim excess batting. Layer backing, batting, and top. Using 1" quilting safety pins, pin the layers together.

Quilt around the flowers and all the details of the floral design. Stipple-quilt the background. Quilt the border as desired. In the sample quilt, I quilted wavy lines around the border about 1" apart.

Trim the edges of the batting and backing even with the border. Bind the quilt. (See pages 79–80 for information on binding.) Make a label and attach it to the back of the quilt. (See page 94 for information on labels.)

Misty Iris
Misty Iris pattern, enlarge 150%

Misty Iris
Misty Iris pattern, enlarge 150%

Designing a Quilting Pattern

There are many templates and books available for marking quilting designs on your quilt tops. However, it can be very satisfying to design your own quilting pattern.

For this method, you will need tracing paper and washable markers, such as those found in the school supplies aisles of discount stores. Tracing paper comes on rolls and in tablets of varying sizes. The paper is available at hobby shops and art supply stores.

Directions

The first step in designing a quilting pattern is to cut a piece of tracing paper that is a little more than one-quarter the size of the quilt. Large quilts are more manageable when worked in smaller sections.

The next step is to mark the quilt's construction lines, such as the block and sashing seams, on the tracing paper. Use a yellow or light color marker for this step.

The quilting pattern should complement and enhance the pieced or appliquéd design. Look at your quilt and ask yourself some questions: Would one of the appliqué flowers or leaves work in the quilting pattern? Can you repeat a shape to fill a plain block area or use it on a border? What about adding some vines? Vines can be drawn by using a draftsman's flexible curve. Lay the tracing drawing on top of your quilt to see if you like the way the design is developing. Shape and re-shape the quilting design until you like the way the design works on your quilt. Grids can also be drawn on the tracing-paper overlay to see how straight-line quilting would look on the quilt top.

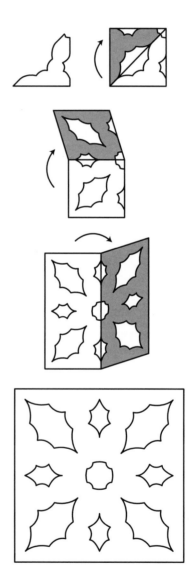

Figure 32. Quilt designs can be developed using paper cut-outs.

If you have a plain, repeat block in your quilt, you can create an original quilting design by folding a piece of tracing paper the size of the block and cutting it into a snowflake pattern (Fig. 32).

When you use tracing paper as an overlay on the quilt top, you can try different designs on the same sheet simply by changing the marker colors.

Once you have the design you like, transfer it to a clean sheet of tracing paper. Trim the tracing paper to size and baste it to the quilt top. Then machine quilt through the paper. When finished, simply tear the tracing paper away from the stitching.

The ideas described here can be used to design original quilting patterns for any quilt you make. Relax and just have fun auditioning quilting designs to use on your quilts. The tracing-paper method can save hours of time because you will be able to see if a particular design will enhance the look of your quilt top before you take a stitch.

Rose Garden
25" x 25"

The Rose Garden consists of one four-block quilt and two one-block quilts. Yardage given will make all three quilts in the grouping. Step-by-step instructions for designing the quilting pattern are included in this project.

Flower Patterns ❋ To Appliqué, Paint, and Embroider   Joan Sjuts Waldman

Rose Garden
17" x 17"

Rose Garden

Fabric Requirements (All yardage based on 45"-wide fabric.)

½ yard bleached muslin for the blocks and inner borders
1¼ yards accent fabric for the outer borders and binding
1½ yards backing for the three quilts
One 27" square and two 19" squares of cotton batting
Scraps or six fat quarters

Cutting Instructions (Cut strips selvage to selvage.)

Painted blocks:

Six 6½" squares of muslin for the rose blocks

Sashing:

Seventy-seven assorted 2½" squares from scraps or fat quarters

Borders:

Five 1½" strips of muslin for the inner borders
Six 3" strips of accent fabric for the outer borders

Finishing:

One 27" square of backing fabric
Two 19" squares of backing fabric
Seven 2¼" strips of accent fabric for the bindings

Directions (Use a ¼" seam allowance for piecing.)

With a fabric pen, trace the rose pattern (page 76) on three of the 6½" blocks and heat set. Trace the rose in reverse on the remaining three blocks. Using the watercolor-pencil painting technique described on pages 6–9, color, wet, dry, and heat set the designs.

Embroider the outlines of the roses and leaves using the stem stitch or chain stitch (Fig. 33).

Assemble the 2½" squares into 10 strips of three squares, three strips of nine squares, and four strips of five squares. Sew the three-square

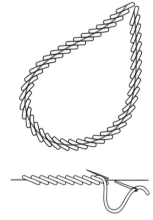

Figure 33. Embroider painted pieces with stem stitch, shown here, or chain stitch shown on page 32.

strips to the sides of the blocks as shown (Fig. 34.) Sew one nine-square strip between the four flower blocks on the large quilt. Then sew the two remaining nine-square strips to the top and bottom (Fig. 35). Sew the four five-square strips to the top and bottom of each small quilt (Fig. 36).

Figure 34. Sew three-square strips to block sides.

Sew the inner border strips on the sides of the quilts. Trim. Press away from the center. Sew the inner border strips on the top and bottom of the quilts. Trim. Press away from the center. Sew the outer border to the sides of the quilts. Trim. Press away from the center. Sew the outer border to the top and bottom of the quilts. Trim. Press away from the center. (Note: Use the remainder of the strips from the large quilt in the small quilts.)

Layer the backing, batting, and top. Using 1" quilting safety pins, pin the layers together.

Figure 35. Sew remaining nine-square strips to top and bottom of large quilts.

Figure 36. Sew five-square strips to top and bottom of small quilts.

Rose Garden

Designing a Quilting Pattern

To design your own quilting pattern for Rose Garden, cut a piece of tracing paper a little larger than one-quarter the size of the quilt.

Mark the quilt's seam lines on tracing paper with a yellow or other light color washable marker.

Begin by tracing the rose in the center of the quilt on another piece of paper. Put the traced rose under the first piece of tracing paper. Using a darker washable marker, trace the rose in one corner of the border and in the center of the border (Fig. 37). You are now ready to decide what to put between the flowers.

Figure 37. Use rose as part of quilting design.

To make a swag between the flowers, use a draftsman's flexible curve. Lay it in place and bend it into a shape that is pleasing to you. Trace the shape. Move the flexible curve a little less than ¼" and trace again to make the shape of a vine between the flowers. Add leaf shapes to the vine by cutting a template the shape of one of the leaves in the quilt design. Trace around the shape as shown (Fig. 38).

Figure 38. Use draftsman's flexible curve to make swags between flowers.

For the small "melon" shape in the muslin border, cut a 1" x 2" piece of graph paper. Fold the paper in fourths and draw a curve (Fig. 39). Cut out the design and use it for your template.

To make the circles in the corners of the inner border, use a compass or draw around a bottle cap.

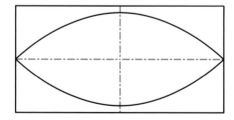

Figure 39. Cut shape for muslin border from quarter-folded paper.

Rose Garden

Quilting and Finishing

Quilt around the center rose, then stipple-quilt around the rose, up to the first border (Fig. 40).

For the pieced border, quilt diagonally across the squares. For the outer border, quilt straight lines approximately 1" apart to finish the quilting (Fig. 41).

Bind the quilt. (See pages 79–80 for information on binding.) Make a label and attach it to the back of the quilt. (See page 94 for information on labels.)

Figure 40. Quilting for rose and pieced border.

Figure 41. Quilting for outer border.

Rose Garden
Full-size pattern

Oversized blocks will be trimmed to 6" after being appliquéd.

Machine Quilting

Machine quilting is a quick and easy way to finish a quilting project. You will use a walking foot to quilt the straight lines. This foot helps the top and middle layers of the quilt to advance at the same pace. You will use a darning foot for free-motion quilting. This foot is used with the feed dogs down or covered. Check your manual to see what your machine requires.

The machine needles I prefer are #70/10, #80/12, or #90/14. Experiment with each size to determine which works best for you. For quilting with metallic thread, I suggest using a special needle available at your fabric store.

The thread you use to quilt with is also a personal decision. Try many different brands until you find one you and your machine like. Invisible monofilament thread can be used as a top thread. This thread comes in clear and smoke. The clear thread is used for light colors and the smoke thread is used for dark colors. The bobbin thread can match the back of the quilt or contrast with the backing. That choice is up to you. My preference for bobbin thread is lingerie and bobbin thread. It is available in black and white. A good-quality thread will make the process easier.

Selecting batting is another personal choice. I prefer a cotton batting with scrim for machine quilting. The scrim seems to keep the batting from shifting as the quilting progresses.

Directions

Assembling the Quilt Before Quilting

Lay the backing on a flat surface. Two or more tables pushed together or a floor work fine. Tape the backing to the surface with masking tape. Smooth the batting over the backing and again tape in place with masking tape. Center the quilt top on the batting and tape in place.

Using 1" quilting safety pins, pin the layers together, about every 4". When the top is completely pinned, remove the tape from the edges and bring the backing over to the front and loosely pin in place. This keeps the batting from catching and tearing while the initial quilting is done.

Machine Quilting

For this, I use the walking foot, with invisible thread on the top and lingerie and bobbin thread on the back. Begin quilting in all the seam lines. This stabilizes the block lines, both horizontal and vertical. Quilt the seams of the borders. Carefully remove the pins from the edge of the quilt and sew a line of stay stitching, ⅛" in from the edge of the last border. Trim the excess backing and batting.

Mark the quilting design on one area of the quilt at a time. Quilt that area. Continue marking and quilting until you have quilted each section. I use a very sharp silver quilter's pencil to mark the design. Mark very lightly. Mark as you quilt. The markings will be almost removed by the time the quilt is complete. What little marking remains will come out with the first washing, or will wear off in a short time. Remember to use a light mark, just enough to see the lines as you quilt. Keep the pencil sharp.

Free-motion quilting the remaining designs can be done more easily if the machine is turned so the head faces you (Fig. 42). The extension tray should be put in place if you have a free arm machine. Drop the feed dogs and put the darning foot in place. Slip the quilt under the needle and begin quilting in the center of the quilt. Place your hands on both sides of the needle and move the fabric smoothly under the needle. The first time you try this position, it will seem very awkward, but stick with it for a while, and I think you will see how well this position works for free-motion quilting.

When the center of the quilt is completed, quilt the borders. Trim the outside edge of the quilt even with the border. Bind the quilt and attach a label.

Check the front side of the quilt to see if any bobbin thread is showing. If some thread is showing, use a fabric pen the same color as the fabric and just apply it to the thread. It will color the thread and eliminate the thread showing on the surface of the quilt.

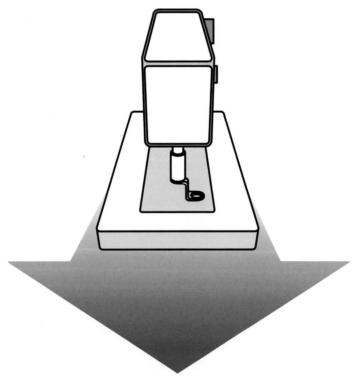

Figure 42.
Free-motion quilting can be done more easily if the head of the machine faces you.

Binding

The following instructions are for a ¼"-wide, straight-grain binding which can be used on any quilt with straight edges. Trim batting and backing even with the edges of the quilt top. Cut 2¼" strips selvage to selvage across the width of the fabric to make the binding. Allow enough strips to go around the quilt plus at least 12 inches.

To join the binding strips, lay two strips, right sides together at a 90-degree angle. Overlap the strip ends ¼". Sew diagonally across the two strips as shown.

Take the opposite end of the top strip and the next strip of binding, and lay them right sides together at a 90-degree angle. Overlap the strip ends ¼". Sew diagonally across the two strips. Continue doing this until all the strips are sewn. Cut the thread between the strips and trim the excess fabric (Fig. 43).

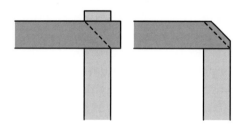

Figure 43. Sew a diagonal seam. Trim, leaving ¼" seam allowance.

Press the binding in half lengthwise, wrong sides together. Press the binding seam allowances open as you come to them. You will notice that the bulk of the seam allowance is spread over a wider area when stitched on the diagonal.

Before you begin sewing, lay the binding around the quilt to see where the seams fall. It can be nearly impossible to get a flat binding in the corner if there is a seam allowance.

Leaving about 12" of binding free, begin stitching along the side of the quilt (Fig. 44). If, when sewing the binding on, you realize you have misjudged the seam placement and know it will end up on one of the corners, stop sewing well before you come to the end. Cut the strip to eliminate the unwanted seam and re-sew the binding to force the seam to fall along the quilt edge.

Figure 44. Leave about 12" of the binding unstitched to allow for joining the ends.

Sew the binding until you are ¼" from the bottom edge of the quilt. Back stitch. Lift the presser foot and pull the quilt from under the foot. Turn the quilt one-quarter turn. Fold the binding straight up at the corner (Fig. 45). Then fold it back down, aligning the raw edge of the binding with the raw edge of the quilt. Begin stitching ¼" from the top edge. Continue until you are ¼" from the bottom edge. Repeat the folds at each of the remaining corners.

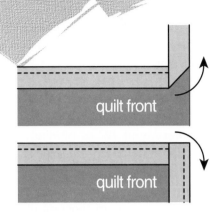

Figure 45. Fold binding up at the corner. Fold binding back down and align with quilt edge.

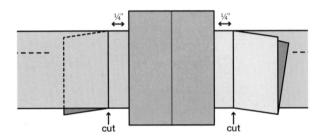

Figure 46. To trim the binding ends to the proper length for joining with a diagonal (45°) seam, use an unfolded piece of binding as a guide. Cut ends ¼" away from edge of guide.

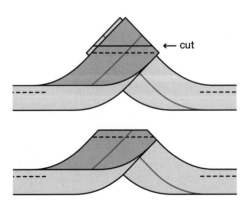

Figure 47. Sew diagonal seam, as in Figure 43, page 79.

To join the ends of the binding, stop stitching about 12" before the ends of the binding meet. Back stitch. Take the quilt from under the presser foot. Lay the two ends of binding so they overlap.

Cut a piece off the end of the binding. About a 2" piece will be sufficient. (This piece of fabric will act as a guide for cutting the ends of the binding.) Unfold that piece of binding and lay it on top of, and perpendicular to, the overlapped binding. Cut the loose ends of the overlapped binding ¼" beyond the edge of the guide piece on either side (Fig. 46). The binding ends now overlap by the width of the binding plus ¼" on either end. Discard the guide piece.

Unfold the ends of the binding. Lay them right sides together at a 90-degree angle. Overlap the binding ends ¼". Sew diagonally as shown. Trim the extra binding, leaving a ¼" seam allowance. Finger press the seam allowance open (Fig. 47). Refold the binding in half lengthwise and finish sewing the binding to the edge of the quilt.

Turn the binding to the back of the quilt and hand stitch in place. Stitch the binding miters closed at the corners (Fig. 48).

Figure 48. Use a blind stitch to sew binding to back of quilt.

Flower Patterns

Most of the flower patterns given were drawn from flowers in my, or my friends' gardens. Others were inspired by various advertisements or seed catalogs. For example, the dogwood block was inspired by a leaflet for the American Quilter's Society show. Ideas are all around you. Learn to see flower shapes and colors, then make a fabric flower garden to enjoy year round.

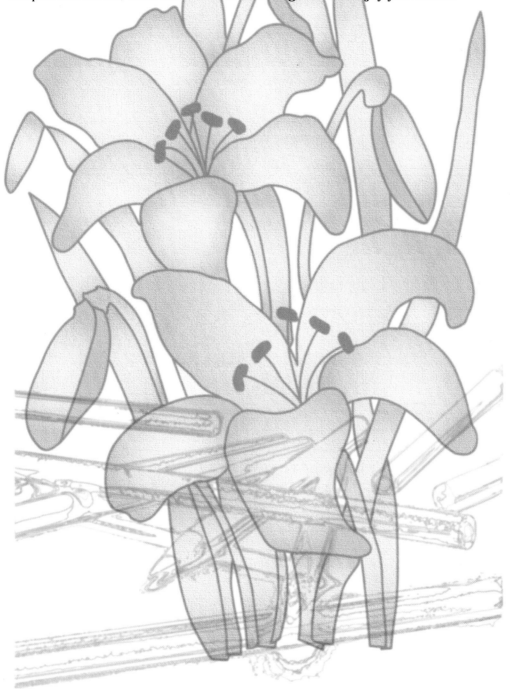

Blue Bells

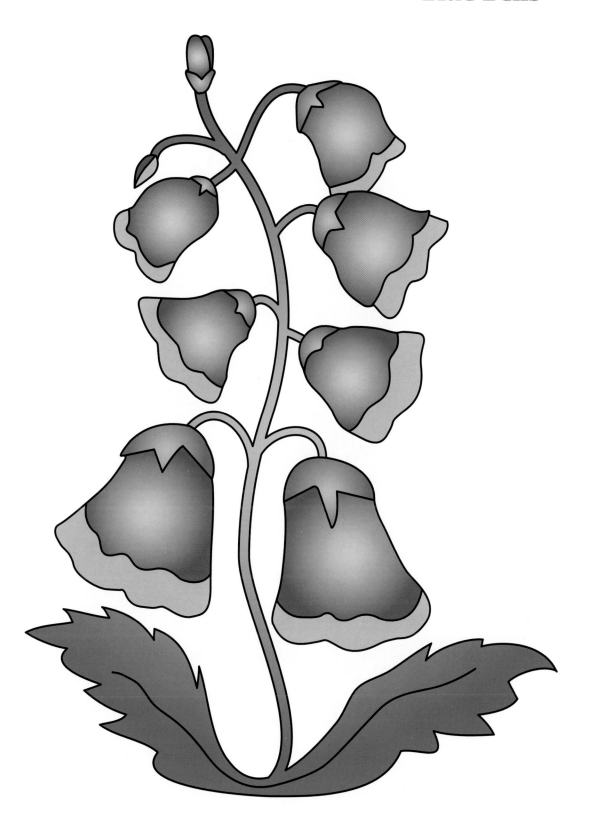

Canterbury Bells

Flower Patterns ✳ To Appliqué, Paint, and Embroider   Joan Sjuts Waldman

Dogwood

Poppies

Roses

Tulips

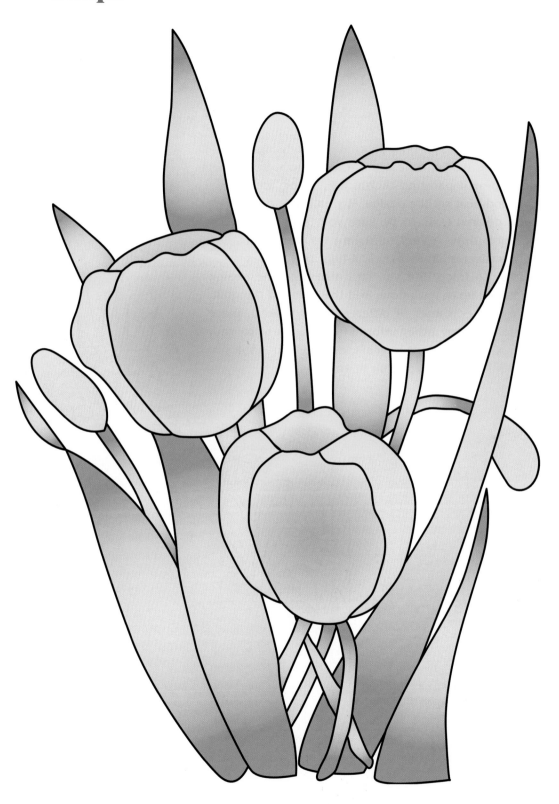

Watercolor-Pencil-Painted Labels

You can make beautiful labels for your quilts using the watercolor-pencil-painting technique described on pages 6–9. Any of the flower patterns in the book can be used to make a label for your quilt.

Enlarge or reduce patterns as needed.

Directions

Trace the design on a piece of fabric using a .01 fabric pen and heat set. Using the watercolor-pencil painting technique, color, wet, dry, and heat set the design. With a fabric pen, print desired text. To be sure your printing is straight, draw a very faint line on the label with a silver quilter's pencil. A light box makes it easy to trace, but you can also hold the design and label up to a window. Add the name of the quilt, date, maker, owner (if different from maker), place made, and any other information pertinent to your quilt. Quilt historians in years to come will thank you for adding this information to your quilt.

Flower Patterns ❋ To Appliqué, Paint, and Embroider   Joan Sjuts Waldman

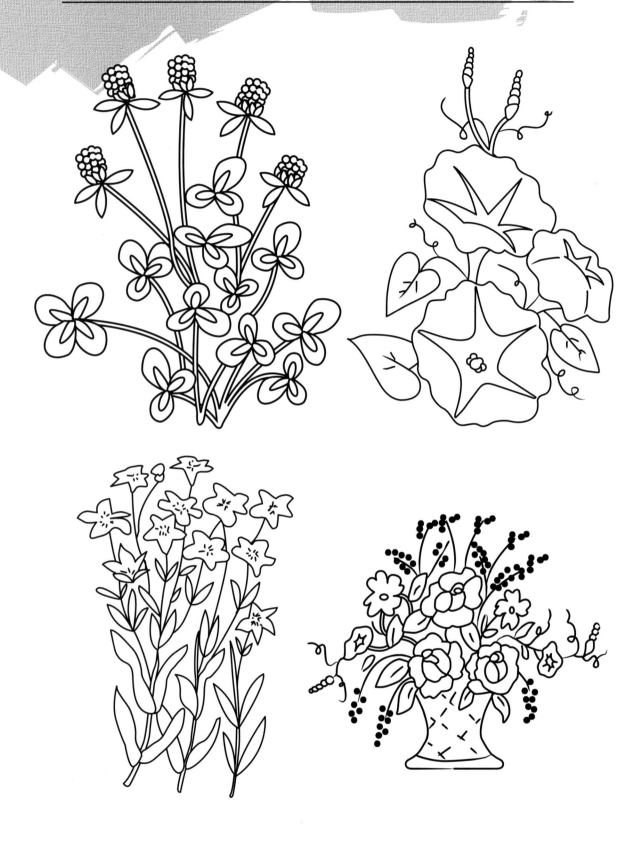

Flower Patterns ✳ To Appliqué, Paint, and Embroider   Joan Sjuts Waldman

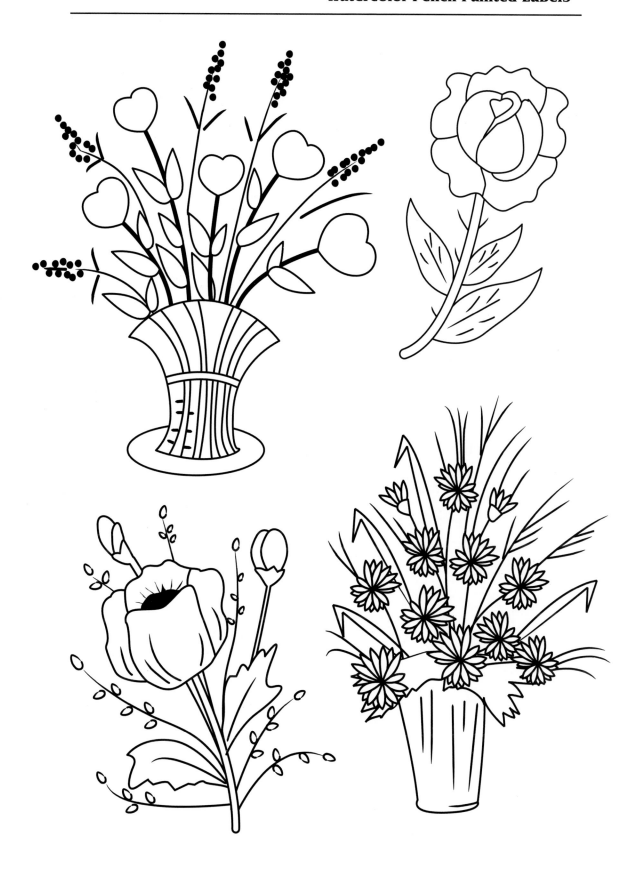

Flower Patterns ❋ To Appliqué, Paint, and Embroider   Joan Sjuts Waldman

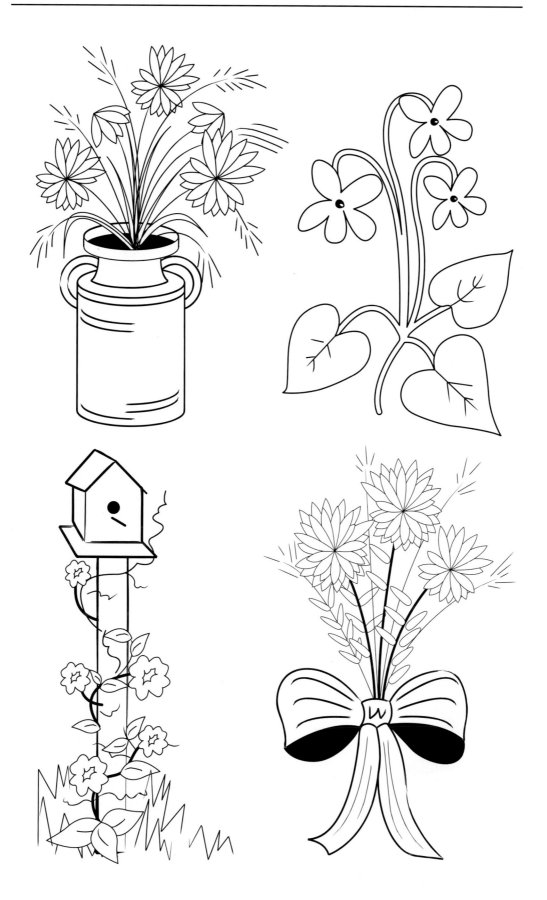

Flower Patterns ✳ To Appliqué, Paint, and Embroider   Joan Sjuts Waldman

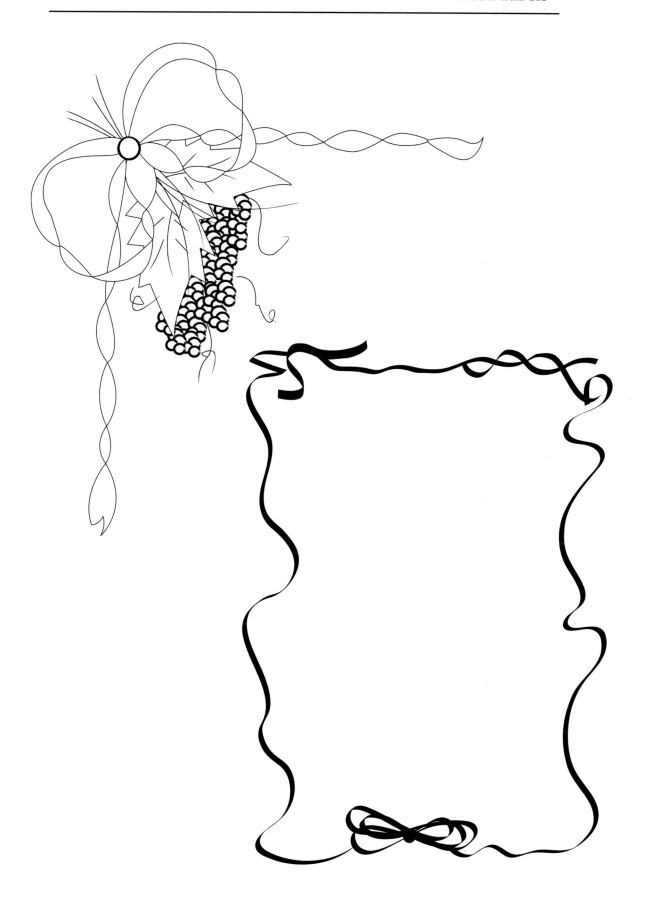

This is only a small selection of the books available from the American Quilter's Society. AQS books are known worldwide for timely topics, clear writing, beautiful color photos, and accurate illustrations and patterns. The following books are available from your local bookseller, quilt shop, or public library.

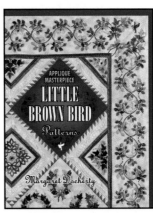

#5335 • $21.95

#5331 • $16.95

#5338 • $21.95

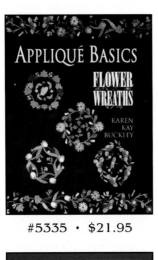

#5012 • $22.95

#5013 • $14.95

#3926 • $14.95

#5382 • $14.95

#5234 • $22.95

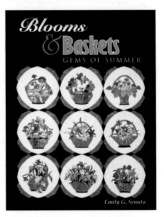

#5175 • $24.95

Look for these books nationally or call 1-800-626-5420